Wisdom's Brief

The Storytells

By Griot (Bosco & KO)

Wisdom's Brief is published under Imagine books, sectionalized division under Di Angelo Publications INC.

IMAGINE BOOKS
an imprint of Di Angelo Publications. Wisdom's Brief. Copyright 2021. Griot in digital and print distribution in the United States of America.

Di Angelo Publications
4265 San Felipe #1100
Houston, Texas, 77027
www.diangelopublications.com

Library of Congress cataloging-in-publications data
Wisdom's Brief. Downloadable via Kindle, iBooks and NOOK.

Library of Congress Registration

Paperback

ISBN: 978-1-942549-78-9

Cover Illustration: Prajwal K Kumar
Interior Illustrations: Prajwal K Kumar
Layout: Kimberly James
Words by: Griot (Bosco & KO)

1. Body, Mind & Spirit --- Inspiration & Personal Growth
2. Poetry --- Subjects & Themes --- General
3. Family & Relationships --- Love & Romance

United States of America with int. Distribution.

Wisdom's Brief

The Storytells

By Griot (Bosco & KO)

Wisdom's Brief is a unique combination of purpose-driven poetry and passion-driven prose, giving voice to a generation of people of color cleaning up the shit that's been flying off the fan. At times biting, painful, and funny, this collection by a performance duo is deeply honest exploring life, work, love, dreams, and faith.

Acknowledgements

To Oko Mi for being a wealth of steady Love and my safest place, to my strong and brave warrior woman (mom) Tracy P, to my pops who challenges me in ways I don't always understand but respect, to the tribe of women that remind me to feel my feminine foolery fully and to all of the beautiful souls who've helped my pieces come together along the way.

-KO

To my brothers, y'all protected me even when I didn't know that I needed a shield. To AV and Willa Bea, the laughter you shared and the tenderness of your bond is forever engrained in my soul. To Michael W, you are more than my uncle, you are also a model I shaped myself after. Most importantly, Rita Lynette (Maaa-Mah). Words of gratitude will never be enough. You are an unflinching force of unwaverable love and I can't say enough how privileged I am to call you my mother. Hopefully this makes up for the cards I forgot.

- Bosco

Prologue

Chapter 1 · That Work Shit

Chapter 2 · That Love Shit

Chapter 3 · That Life Shit

Chapter 4 • That Dream Shit

Chapter 5 - That Faith Shit

PROLOGUE
Blessing's Bridge

I think I may get laid off. Annnd I'm lowkey excited. I think this may be the push I need. To finally pursue all of me to the best of me because there would be no other recourse. It's hard for me to just implement LEAVE. This job has been such a blessing. It came out of nowhere, at a time when I was in desperate need. My "Spaces of Living" checks could only handle but so many more "tax removals", knowing that at some point the government was coming to get theirs. But also knowing I would have nothing to give the government. I'd dug a necessary hole with no ladder to climb out. I was scared. Didn't know what options I could take. I was determined to not rely on family although I have it here in abundance in this city in which I chose to relocate. I'd made the decision to move from my life to my life to make my way and I could NOT allow familial dependency. I refused to!

Finances became more constrained. Living alone in LA is not cheap. I pondered options. Rent my couch? Maybe. But I honestly didn't want another roommate situation after the horror that was my first one. Uber and convenience delivery weren't a thing yet and at that time there wasn't an abundance of jobs. The economy was on a slow incline. Each day I took as it came. Simply believing blessings come when blessings come. Sometimes patience is all that's needed and of that I have plenty. Going back home was not an option and despite my fears of financial instability, here is where I knew I would remain, because here is where I knew I needed to be to discover me and become "Me" in all my glory.

My storm of concern ended while processing the return of a rug and an issue with some incomplete end tables (I worked in furniture at the time). At my then place of employment whenever an individual walked up to the counter to deal with their customer service problems all of the supervisors looked at one another before getting up. Pretty much gauging who was next to deal with yet another bad news scenario. That's customer service. We fix what was broke and nothing is worse than your new shit being broken and you didn't break said shit.

The day was slow. It was midweek. My staff was small. The other head lead on duty was engaged in another issue, so this well-dressed man that appeared to be returning an expensive rug was my responsibility. He was on the phone, which in my mind meant he was already to be annoying and rude because it's hard to discuss what one needs when they are already having a discussion with someone else. In my experience in dealing with other well-dressed men wrapped up in their phones, they tended to have an air of self-importance that I loathed. So my "I bet I'm going to have to show this dude he isn't any better than anyone" guard was already up.

But to my surprise as I strolled to the counter and called him forward, he got off his phone. "Ok" I said internally. My guard went to half-mast. It wasn't gone however, because I was waiting on that "entitled" comment, but it never came. My mast of defense had all but disappeared. He explained what he needed, which was to return his rug and how his salesman had only sold him half of the materials to make the tables whole. Which meant he would have to pay for the rest of the other halves. Knowing that I would have to deliver that news the mast went up a fourth, but even after hearing that he just said "ok" and paid. He was so nice, so I was extra nice (side note: don't treat your customer service reps like they're the ones who messed up your stuff. If you do, and cuss them out, blame them or be rude or aggressive toward them, they will really mess your stuff up or tell you it is out of stock, or delay your shit because they WILL do that and do it with a smile ...I did!).

As the transaction ended however, he was so happy with the service I provided he complimented me on my service etiquette. And this is where I was blessed. He offered me a job in the very office that the rug and tables were furnishing.

I often wonder where I would be if I'd not gone to work that day or just not been able to work on his order. But I did. I was meant to. After a month of interviews my non-degree-having ass was able to secure a job at a media firm listed in Forbes. Two years past half a decade later, I am still here thriving. In a way, he saved my life and I am forever grateful, and I don't take lightly that grace. But office space has never been my taste.

In these immediate recent years, the walls began to close. Now this part is all my fault. I pulled back on my own creative endeavors because I knew it wouldn't work with work. Then that evil thing called complacency settled in my being. I now could live alone as I wanted and live comfortably. All the while knowing deep down, I wanted far more than three and half walls of cubicle space.

I am extravagant (which is perfectly ok to proclaim about yourself). But also thinking don't you be a fool and just walk out on your blessing, on that grace. That'd be a slap in the face. So I stayed...stayed comfortable and created less. But turmoil began to loom. Bad business practices lead to unwanted— but needed— downsizing. It seemed my choice to just stay comfortable might not be left in my hands. I may just have to acclimate to life again. Which I know I can do...I'd done it before, and I am prepared to do it again. I now realize this blessing, this grace given to me was the bridge from my struggle to my actual destiny.

CHAPTER ONE
That Work Shit

The Chase

For some people it's cut and dry; there is no other option. They just are who they are, period. They don't pursue any other avenue, because for them there is no other avenue to take. The only one there is, is the one that they are on. And if, for some God forsaken reason, that road blocks, so does their life... and it takes them a while to detour and get around. But when they do get around, they get right back on their road even if they are off of it for some time. The motivation is that they know the detour will take them to the road they've traveled their whole life. The road that has always made sense.

Now the detour sucks—well, initially. You have no idea where you are, or maybe you do but you've never used this road for this long. Maybe just to cut traffic, or to get around, or just in crossing...but, you've never actually driven down the road this long. This detour feels a lot like failure. Although there are signs that reassure that you're in the right place and going the right way, it doesn't feel right. It doesn't feel safe. It doesn't feel like anything you've felt before and even though you see those signs you question it. You are so unsure of how this vaguely familiar road could lead you back to your path that you blindly trust the signs. You don't have a choice. I mean, you could not trust the signs. You could try to figure it out on your own and end up probably taking a lot longer or doing damage to yourself or others.

Or trust the detour. And after the initial shock, you find things on this detour that actually make you smile. You actually WANT to be there. And for all purposes, you tell yourself to relax. You note things to remember later. You start to enjoy the detour. And right when you start to get comfortable you realize that the detour is coming to an end and you have to return to the road you've always traveled. The road that has defined you your entire life. And part of you is anxious, maybe even hesitant. Because that's the nature of change. It calls us to the unfamiliar. It calls us to the unknown. It calls us to the untapped.

And because we fear what we don't know, change is terrifying. Because in every change there is an unfamiliar, unknown, untapped element that we must face. And I've been running from mine. The more I run, the more it chases. If I run faster, it runs faster. If I slow, it slows some but not enough. Its presence threatens my comfort, threatens my routine, my...well my world as I know it. Because it is coming to change me. To change my world. See, when you're being chased by change it seems incredibly scary. In fact, scarier than it actually is. And when you chase after something, know that it will run; if it is a worthy catch. It's not going to sit still; it will make you work.

So, I stopped running away from change and started running period. You see, it wasn't the running that was bad, it was the drive for the run. Fear can't be my drive anymore. It can ride in the backseat, but it cannot drive. It cannot be in the front, it has too much influence. So now I'm running. Because before, my running was actually me chasing comfort, chasing security, chasing familiarity. Chasing the known. And in that chasing, I was running away from change. But change was not going to stop until it caught me. You see it only slows because change will not force itself. It will simply get close. And closer. And closer. As close as we allow until it catches and takes us with it towards the unfamiliar. Towards the unknown, towards the untapped element that we must face, head on.

The nature of chasing

Have you ever chased after something?
Wondering why the more you chase it the more it runs?
Wondering why it seems as though you could never catch it?
And even if you did, you'd be too tired to do anything with it?
Well that's the nature of chasing.
If you chase it, it will run.

And it runs fast
Faster than you expected
Too fast to catch it
This feels wrong
But how does one correct it
When that's the nature of chasing
If you chase it, it will run.

And it runs long
Longer than you expected
And the gap becomes
A sea, no, ocean of
A thing that once was
Or things that once were
Swallowed by the waves
Of change
That I can't tame
But that's the nature of chasing
If you chase it, it will run.

I'm done.
I'm tired.

Exhausted by the chase
Challenged by the weight
Of the wait
When I just want to take it
Maybe what needs to change is my impatience?
Or my unrealistic expectations?
Chasing wind

That Work Shit

that shifts directions
frequent
can't see it
just going off of my feelings
that change just as frequent
but am I willing to see
all of the wonderful things chasing me?
Maybe I need to stand still
Or better yet

Run.

Run with purpose
Knowing that if I run
Life will chase me
Catch and take me
On journey's path
Where I'll have
What I perceive as lack
No more back
And forth
No more tag
I'm it!
I'm running
And Life is Chasing
For that is the nature of chasing
If I run, Life will chase me
Catch and take me
On journey's path

The Breaks

I guess I've been sittin' in a box
Hopin' that somehow it just unlocks
Without me rockin' it
Without me shakin' it
Cause I don't wanna shake
My comfort zone but
I don't want this spot to be my home
So
I breakout.

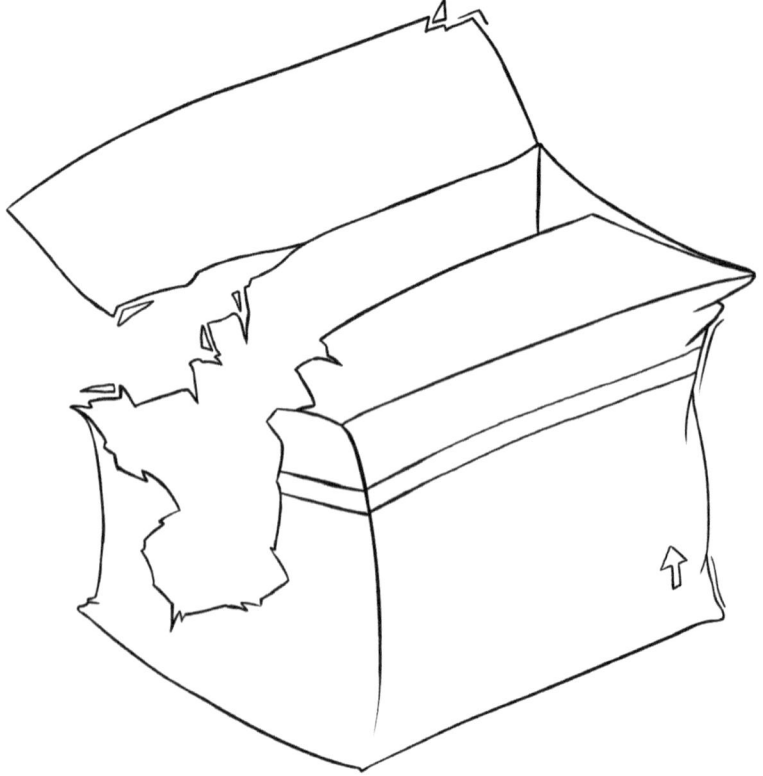

Breaking Broken

I think I'm done being broken
It was cool for a bit
And the attention I'd get
Was fit for a queen
But attention at the expense of my well being
Isn't worth its weight in gold

And it's heavy
But so is healing
Heavy is the weight of both
But only one helps me reach the goal
So I push my plow
In the now
Not the past or future
I don't need to know the how
I just trust it'll all work out

And it does
I'll no longer attract who I was
I'll attract who I am
And as I vibrate
At a higher frequency
I heal me
And healing can be heavy
But I'm ready

<u>Self-Love</u>

If I'm honest, I'm my biggest critic
I've said things to me
You wouldn't dream of.
Because I'm still learning love...
Me...
Learning to love me
The good bad and the ugly.

Untitled

I'm a bully and apologetic to everyone else for it. I.E. I walk in a room and say sorry for walking a bit slow...no one is behind me and no one is waiting on me except me. So, my sorry to them is unsolicited and misplaced like a politician's sign in your front yard or a probe inserted ANYWHERE at the doctor's office. It makes sense to no one but the bully inside of me and everyone is just happy I'm there...the bully, however, has served his purpose and pushed me down yet again. Now every joke or slightly ambiguous remark is an insult hurled at me (not really) and another notch lower in my self-esteem (that I pushed down) smh the trickery of self-bullying (delusion).

Here's what self-bullying is: this incredibly painful and awkward dance of vulnerability that we numb (with some innocent at first but incredibly unhealthy coping mechanism) and excuse (bully) the truth out of until we are left staring at the lies we've either created or believed. Either way, we empowered those lies...they literally can't function without our energy.

Here

Sometimes
Not even I understand
It's not like I plan to spazz
Nobody plans to spazz
It's a reaction
A flick of the neurons
A trick of the nuance

And that's just it
The little shit
That we don't actually see
Until these
Little baby blow ups reveal things
Tiny little fragments left from trauma's past
Engrafted in our current
Our turbulent flow
From woes, and foes and those things that throw our rhythm

And ear drums play over and over
The self-deprecating lyrics that quench our spirit

In Layman's terms:

Shit you've said still plays in the back of my mind
And I find it on loop like a sound bed for my head
Of weaved web spinning me round and round
Until sound stops
And beats flop
And melodies disappear
And now all I hear are these words

That still hurt in places I numbed
Trying to mute you
But somewhere I hear "this pain doesn't suit you.
Feel it and free your spirit."

That's real healing

But am I ready to set that series of scenes in motion...?
Here's hoping.

Move

I don't know what I want.
I do know what I can handle.
I can handle it all.
Certainly, the good that comes with, but also the unavoid-
able bad.
The hardships. Even the unknowns I can handle.
I'm built of that fray.
I was taught that way.
To not just fall down and be below, but up you get and to
fight
through until you are back.
Back to good.
Voyaging to the precipice of great.
I don't know what I want.
I doubt my beliefs.
Time heals the wounded.
Unfortunately, this scar is permanent.

However, "I don't know" is progression.
A year ago, I was more aligned with the "Niggas Ain't Shit"
mentality.
But despite the reinforced titanium safe with 10-inch steel
walls encased in polycarbonate I placed myself in, there was
still that nagging desire for intimacy.
Not sex, but intimacy. Defined as closeness, familiarity, com-
panionship. That want I could not shake and that "N.A.S."
mentality I allowed to become
I'm open, but not seeking
An advance in my stance I just knew would never come.

So a spark was lit in an unexpected but refreshing and
probably needed way. Question is...do I have the ability to
let those embers rage?

Sincerely,
Progressively Stagnant

It

There are people who grow up knowing exactly what they want to be.

They may not know exactly how to get there, but they know what "it" is.

Like they were born with "it."

Like "it" grew up with them, shared a room with them as kids and walked to school with them as preteens.

Like "it" knew all of their stories.

Their first kiss, their first dance, their first fight, their first flight, their first love and their first heartbreak.

Their first drink, their first smoke, their first lie and their first choke.

"It" knew all of the intimacies and "it" knew in detail.

"It" is so much a part of them that you sometimes forget they are two.

They're like a perfect union.

When you see them, you know "it" is not far behind.

And they make such a good pair.

"It" grows with them.

"It" teaches them things and takes them into depths they didn't know existed.

"It" drives them into the best version of them self and gives them a place to be...

well...

just be.

"It" is so tangible, so present.

Yet somehow, I think mine got lost.

Or maybe "it" didn't want to be as close.

Or maybe "it" is and I'm just in denial.

Maybe I know exactly what "it" is...

But if I know you...

Why can't I name you?

Headstrong

Mental strength controls alllllll of the things. It will access the coach (that inner voice) you've been listening to. It will access all thoughts applicable to a situation. It will access emotions to back up whichever voice and line of thoughts it decides to support and follow. Don't believe me? Test the theory. Lay on the ground and lift your legs just barely off the ground. (they should be floating in the air but not way up, just hovering over the ground) and do the same with your arms. Hold it for as long as you physically can and then hold it for another twenty seconds. Some of you were done at the twenty extra seconds like "naw bruh, I'm not doing nothing extra!" Some of you were out at the going as long as you physically can like "when it starts to hurt, I'm done!" Some of you were out at hovering your legs over the ground lol. I laugh because this is exactly what my trainer told me once.

Mind you I was in no way physically strong enough to just hold my legs and arms out for a long time. In fact, the first time we did this exercise I failed miserably.

He said, "Alright go."

I lifted my legs and arms and grimaced thinking oh my gosh, oh my gosh! Because as soon as I lifted both arms and legs, I felt the pull on my weak core to hold up my limbs.

My poor core was like "STOP IT RIGHT NOW!!! You haven't worked me! I'm not strong!"

So, guess what happened? I dropped those legs and arms as soon as that pain message was sent to my brain. And because I hadn't exercised mental strength (my mind telling my body what to do) I was done! You hear me? Lol

My trainer is steady trying to coach me saying, "Come on Komica you can do it, come on, pick your legs back up, do it."

I looked at him and said the two words that assassinate mental strength.

"I can't!"

Now I expected him to do one of two things: yell at me like a drill sergeant until I did what I was told or move on from the workout disappointed because I didn't try (Big shot out to you, B, because you never let me walk away disappointed! you helped change my life! :D). You know what he did y'all? He laid down beside me and said five words out of shape people (be it mental, emotional, spiritual or physical) hate to hear.

"Yes you can, just try."

I'm thinking "I JUST DID!!!" I wasn't trying to hear the "yes we can" speech. But it was harder to be angry and hateful with him being all nice and supportive. I kind of wanted him to get mad to give me a reason to quit. But he didn't. Can you believe that?

He told me to try again. Mind you, this is not the beginning of the workout! I had been putting in work for the last hour and my body was SUPER tired!

He kept saying, "Come on, Komica just try."

To which I'd reply, "I've been trying B, I'm not great at this, I just can't."

Do you know what he had the nerve to say?

"I'm not asking you to be great, I'm asking you to try and when you give it your best and you finish, that will be great."

WHAAAAAAAAAAAT! Did you hear that Jedi mind trick he just pulled on me?!?! Talkin' about just try and my trying and finishing will be great, HA! Now that's how my mind responded initially (defensively). But He followed that truth with the secret weapon. He pulled out the big guns y'all: encouragement. COME ON MAN!

He saw the "I give up" look on my face. He knew I was tired

because he was the one pushing me to do all of this crazy stuff! BUT, he also knew that I was much stronger mentally than I knew and he intended to show me that strength.

So he said, "Listen, you are much stronger than you know, give yourself a chance."

Now I'd heard that before so that didn't hit me all that hard, but the next line did.

"I'm right here with you, I've got your back."

NO. HE. DIDN'T.

Now he wants to offer support and stuff?! A little part of my heart spoke up loudly and said:

"It's ok!!!"

But my brain didn't agree! So now I'm having a mini war with my head and my heart. My mind is saying:

"Girl if you lift these legs up and they collapse just as soon as you try then we fail! And we are not about to fail, uh uh, not in front of him!"

To which my heart replied "but he said he has our back, he's going to support us, it's ok! If we fail, he'll help us! He said he's right there with us!"

And y'all know where my mind went.

"People have said that before and they've let us down! Don't believe the hype heart! Now, we did our best that's all he can expect!"

To which my heart replied "Did we? Did we really do our very best or did we just try really hard? Come on, one more time that's it he said that it was the trying and completing that made us great, not trying to be great at doing this."

Doesn't this happen all of the time? This internal warfare? It's like watching a debate between two very knowledgeable people with two very different strategies! It's intriguing and each argument is convincing! Like watching a really close game, both teams are scoring points which one will win? Well that's the problem actually...

Collide

(To come together with violent, direct impact)

I can't do this anymore...
one's on my left, one on my right
one says walk away, the other screams "fight"
I sit wondering which one's right
because this plight
happens all the time
it's a war between my heart and mind
I find
they seldomly agree
they both want to be free
but which one knows what's best for me
collide...
because inside this war is raging
and I'm caged in
can't show the world the breakin'
game face on
but all day long
I'm trying hard to choose
which voice to heed, who to listen to
which way to go love and peace, war and truth
collide...
but I hide
because tears break my stride
can't move forward I feel the weight of life
pulling on my soul
pulling on my whole
now broken pieces coat
my inner man
how can I win
this war, a dead end
collide...
the voice grows stronger

the whisper now seems to linger a little longer
telling me to win you must give in
give in to me
give in to free
mind body and soul collide, complete
I know it feels weak
but in your weak, I create meek
strength in control, strength wrapped in peace
the greatest strength you can be
trust me...
so, I'm trusting
praying for collision
heart and mind
combine
no more solo decisions
consult one another, you both got my back
no one greater than the other
humility keeps us on track
and when you align
I find
peace, love and life
so, *Collide*
because
sometimes I'm emotional
other times I'm rational
trying to choose which way to go
realizing now I need both
to be rationally emotional is free
one word sent the answer to my soul's cry
collide
don't have to worry Cause love's churning inside
collide
and when love's done
my heart and mind decide to
COLLIDE

Now to all those that are well all of the time this might not apply. But for those of us that get a little "off" sometimes this is where it gets a little tough to exercise that mind, adjusting perception. Widening the lens so you can see with your heart as well as your mind, which sometimes is not even an argument because they see the same thing the same exact way! But a lot of times since the mind and heart are driven by different things—logic and emotion, respectively—they don't always agree with how to deal with what is seen. Especially since the mind (logic) is like an older sibling to the heart (emotion), it's always trying to protect the heart.

Your mind (logic) will want to protect your heart (emotion) because it's wired to do so. But that's where your soul (will and core) comes in to help adjust things. Your spirit, like a parent, steps in and says, "Alright, alright enough arguing. This is what we're doing. Ok?" And on that note, let's go back to the trainer and me!

The thought of pushing myself to do more already made my muscles hurt! And the fact that I had been pushing myself all this time and that I was tired made me believe, "Hey my muscles are done, they might give out on me." All facts! All true. But...Well let me just finish the story :)

I really just wanted more than anything for my trainer to stop pushing (the right) buttons. In the middle of his extended encouragement, I rudely interrupted.

"All right, all right! I'll try, but if I don't do it, I already told you I couldn't." (defensively)

He was cool and calm.

He simply replied, "Alright, on the count of three, legs and arms up, ready?"

I wanted to say, "NO WE'RE DONE HERE!" but I just nodded my head and closed my eyes, anticipating the fail. He counted down and I lifted my legs and arms with all the energy I had left in me. I could hear him saying, "Hold it, hold it come on Komica hold it up!"

Annnnd fail! My legs dropped just as quick as I put them up and I immediately yelled, "SEE! I told you!"

He simply said, "Come on, try again, you can do it, you're strong."

I replied, "No I'm not! My core can't do anymore, and my leg muscles are beyond hurt!"

He smiled (another Jedi mind trick!) and said, "Use your mind. Tell yourself you can do it, and you will."

My first thought was "really?!" But I couldn't help but smile because he was smiling at me.

"You ready?"

Again, with that ready question. I just shook my head and smiled.

"1, 2, ready GO!"

I was grunting, yelling, face was all scrunched up legs and

arms shaking, abs burning, sweat dripping into my eyes...I was a mess! (don't act like you haven't had this moment in the gym!) When he got to the end of the ten count, I was ready to drop my legs and then he had the nerve to say, "Ten more seconds, come on Komica DIG!"

I was shocked. I couldn't think of anything good to say to him (nor did I have the energy to say anything negative) I thought "FINE!" But it was fine fueled by frustration, so it came out like this

"AHHHHHHHHHHHHHHHHH!"

And to my surprise (and I think his...though he'll never admit it!) I held it ten more seconds and then collapsed. I was breathing so hard that I scared my trainer!

He joked like "don't die on me!"

We both laughed, he high fived me and helped me off the ground. It hurt like crazy and I shook and screamed like I was being electrocuted, BUT I finished. I did it. My mind told my abs to hold my legs up despite the pain, despite the fatigue, and they did. I was stronger than I knew; my trainer was right! He knew, but I had just figured it out. I'd just seen the proof. Well guess what? (I'm waiting for you to say what)

So are you.

Yeah, I said it. Because you are, you just haven't seen it yet. You haven't pushed pass the pain yet. You've been listening to every past failure and mistake. Every hurt, accusation, label, doubt, and the facts are stacking against you. They present a very strong case against you. I know pain is real, and pain is crippling. Pain can stop you dead in your tracks and keep you from ever trying, ever reaching, ever attempting. And all you know how to do is react, because responding requires your mind and heart to work together and that requires exercise... and that hurts...I know it hurts.

But aren't you just a tiny bit curious to know what's on the other side of pain? What's on the other side of hurt? What it would feel like to respond and not react to everything? What it would feel like to breathe in and out normally unrestricted instead of holding your breath inadvertently all the time? You are so much stronger than you think. Ask me how I know? Because strength is not something you have or don't have, it's something you develop. The question isn't if you're strong, you are. The question is who are you listening to? Fear or Faith? Love or Hurt? Pain or Purpose? Who is training you?

MINEself

Clearly you each thought I was playing.
I certainly understand your position and appreciate your
concern, because yes, I am spurned.
Never not admitted that.
The lack of interest is truly real.

It's my choice.
One that I myself acknowledge as unfortunate but do deem
necessary.
In truth, it's not worth it to me.
We live in an age where asking someone to rest their mobile
device long enough to devote themselves to conversation can
cause a rift between relations. Where fantasy and façade and
created realities are more important to one's actual actuality.
Drowning in their shallowness, desperate for clicks, clawing
for significance, simply to feel loved.
In some cases, even when they already are.

Or is it really to be loved.
I myself have fallen prey to that trap.
We scroll for hours wasting time, viewing life instead of living it.
This social connection is ripping us apart.
We don't value one another, stuck in our created worlds,
the micro and macro. We value the show and I'm no longer
interested in purchasing a ticket.

I am liberal in thinking but conservative in thought.
My values apparently now abstract.
Monogamy and sole devotion seem to be outlandishly fraught.
Building rather than pitching tents.
Foundation.

But not today.
The mentality seems to be, "I'm happy...Like really happy...This
is happy?...You know I've never felt happy like this..But I think I
could be happier?"

That Work Shit

And on that note, I'm good. It sucks I know, sad it's true. I concede all. And if this relational disdain incapacitated my movements.
Kept me cowering in woefulness, I could rock with your notions of unease.
But I am not...cowering
Handled my shit is being. Thriving, I am truly seeing. I am good and fine with my state.

Truly Mineself
Signed,
Uninterested

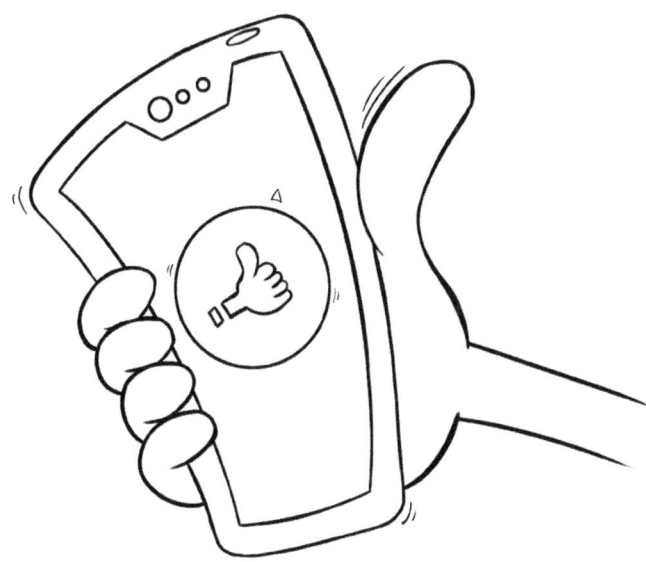

<u>Uncovered</u>

If you're going to leave me
Let me help you
Cut you off at the root
Free you from the place you've held
My whole life

We haven't always agreed
We've fought
You've won
I've lost
We've tied
And I've tried
To hide you
Tame you
Arrange you to fit me

But pain has pushed you to be free
From me
From the place you've held my entire life
And this hurts
And I'm torn
Because you've defined me

That Work Shit

But as I free you, you remind me
I am
Whether you crown me or not
I am royal
I am grateful

You didn't leave me disabled
You left me fully capable
Maybe a bit unsure
A bit insecure
A bit peculiar
A lot of unfamiliar

I embrace this new smooth terrain
You've left
I feel the wind
I feel the chill and the heat
I feel the beat pulsing through me
An intensity
I never felt when you covered me

<u>Breaking Blah</u>

I'm getting to a place where I don't have to have you

Like I won't stop breathing eating or sleeping because you abandoned ship

I realize that this is more about I than us

And there's more than meets the eye if we trust it

If I trust it

Plan...adjustments

Land, Impact,

It's that simple.

Now dimples deepen where frowns lived

Now grace is lived in

Now faith is strengthened

Now life is lengthened

Now soul is stirred and purged of guilt

of hurt

of his of hers

Possessed by none, loved by God

Freed by love for me, thru me

Truly free

It's a scary thing

But discipline will be my guide as I stride through it...

Just like rhythm in music

<u>Visible</u>

My body is a perfect analogy for my deepest desire and how it manifests. My deepest desire(personally) is to be seen, not like physically to see me. I know people see me, but for a good part of my life they didn't see me. Ok...let me just get to the analogy so this can make sense (I hope). There are certain muscles and bone structures that I LOVE. Like legit love. In this order: Sternocleidomastoid (muscle), clavicle (bone), latissimus dorsi (muscle), and the external obliques (muscle). When I can see these on people, holy crap! I get super excited. For a bit of background: I'm a healthcare major, and I had to take a lot of 'study the body' classes like anatomy and physiology. Anatomy lab (where we worked on actual bodies) was my FAVORITE! I loved seeing how things worked, how they were attached, and dissecting...it was all soooooooo dope to me. Like I get 'kid in a candy store' excited. I ALWAYS see them on people, and when they are prominent, I get EXTRA excited.

When I look at myself...I don't see it, but I know they are there because I know they exist on every human. I have proof of that. I want people to see them on me (at this point in my health journey my clavi's and sternocleidomastoid are pretty prominent). But they can't and they don't...they don't even try.

It's not their fault though, because I'm asking them to see something that not even I see. I just know they are there. I can't see them. And instead of doing the work to expose them to unearth them, to make them visible, I appreciate them in others and make a big deal about how dope it is, Silently wishing they'd see it on me or at least see where it would be if it was visible.

Silly me, I was putting the responsibility of being visible on the eyes of, hell anyone... and it is NOT their responsibility. Let me say that again "my visibility is NOT their responsibility."

A Little Trip

If I had a lotta money
And a lotta time then I'd
Take a little trip around the world
Yeah, I'd take a little trip

But my money's funny and my time is tight so I
Close my eyes for a bit
And I quiet my mind for a split
Sec and...lift

Lift up my mind
Yeah
Lift up my heart yeah
Lift up the parts of me that got me feeling low

Feeling the vibe
Feeling the light
Yeah
Letting my mind show me the pictures I can't see
And I rise to the frequency of love

Love for myself
Love for others

<u>Hollow</u>

I told my pragmatist/realist self that "love" is not worthy of you. Because the world does not love as you do.

Unlearning

I've lived my life as an apology
To anyone and everything that had an
Expectation of me
An opinion rather
That they used to abuse the
Boundaries I weakly put in play

But it's the dawning of a new day

I am in the process of
Changing my mind
And I find
That as it transforms
I am over the pleasing for approval
Because I am a magnet
So, attraction is habit
And somehow, I've managed to attract
The good
So, imagine the great that is on its way
Because I stopped playing safe
And started playing point.

Insecurities

They rise
Quicker than heartbeats on
Adrenaline

They scream
Louder than microphones with
Interference

They take
All of the space left
Unoccupied

And I
Have decided
There are no vacancies

Little Things

I learned something about myself today. Like something very simple...I don't like bugs. That's putting it lightly, I HATE bugs like to the point of paralytic fear. Like my only thought when I see one is fight or flight. That decision depends on how big and how much fear I have of it. The more scared I am the more I go into fight, the more I don't know about the bug the more I go into flight. Enter me at the flat I share with my husband in Lagos. I woke up before him with waaaay too much energy, so I hopped up out the bed...took a look in the mirror and said...

"Whew bih you need to shower!" (I forgot to take my makeup off the night before, so I looked a little haphazard... smh)

I walk out of the bathroom to grab things to shower but couldn't focus because the flat was a MESS. We were a little tipsy the night before. So, I decided to straighten up the place first so that I wouldn't sweat out my fresh shower, ya feel me? Because remember, this is African heat so, the sweat game is SUPER REAL! I start to clean up, picking up this, folding that, putting away this. I grab the broom to sweep up the sand we drug in from the beach when...

"What did we leave on the wall?! That's a big black mark! Did we rub something against it? Wait...is it mov...oh shoopy doopy!"

I freeze. Literally paralyzed in fear because I realize this is a bug. A big 'ol bug of unknown species! I have no idea what it is, I just know it's big and moving slow on this wall. I immediately start sweating. Every muscle in my body is tense because I want to run, but this is my house!

"What you won't do, lil' ass bug, is run me out of my house!"

...It's just talk. The only reason I didn't run is because there was nowhere but outside to run to and I'm not super familiar with outside sooooo, nope!

I stand there for about five minutes staring at the bug while also low-key trying to coach me into action because I need to finish cleaning so I can shower before they take the water! (yeah that's a thing. They take all kinds of stuff in Lagos: water, light...). I hear my husband stirring in bed and I feel relief run through my body, whew! He'll save me! He'll kill the bug; he doesn't mind stuff like this! But he just stirs and goes back to sleep. I'm devastated! And low-key feeling like he left me out to dry (PS. ...he didn't do anything wrong lol). So, I start trying to make a little more noise in the house while still keeping my eye on this bug, so it doesn't move out of my sight. I'm opening trash bags I don't need, sweeping HELLA loud, bumping into things unnecessarily, dropping things on "accident" and BOOM! He wakes...for two seconds and goes back to sleep. Guys, I wasted like 20 minutes

doing this nonsense only to have to face this damn bug myself, all by myself.

I start coaching myself.

"Come on Ko, if you were the only one here, you'd HAVE to do it."

"But I'm not the only one here!"

"Stop it! You will not wake this man because you're scared to grab a shoe and smash a bug! Come on! That bug is waaaaay smaller than you, grab that shoe and leggo! You got this!"

"But what IS it?! What if it has wings?! What if when I go to hit it, it flies up in my space?! I will die...I will literally die of shock."

"Why are you so dramatic lol? You will not die; you're just scared and that's ok. Carry your scary ass over to that flip flop grab it and leggo!"

"Ok...ok...you're right".

I walk over to grab my shoe but mine felt too small, so I grabbed my husband's size 13's...more reach means I don't have to get as close! I walk slowly towards the bug. I have the oozy in my hand, ready to fire. I get about three feet within range and my stomach does a backflip.

"Aw man! I can't."

"You can and you will!"

"It's going to..."

"Shhh shh shhh, just kill it, you've spent enough time what if-ing."

"Ok...ok."

I walk back over to my three-foot range I close one eye so I can aim well. Line up the shoe and do a few practice swings. I feel good about my chances of hitting this bug on the first shot. I'm getting confident. (Mind you, this bug hasn't moved throughout this entire now thirty-minute ordeal.)

"Ok Ko, you got this..."

I walk up closer now, two feet in range I aim...get my shot lined up...and...

"Oyyyyye!" I yelp and back off of the bug because it's moving its little antennas and I can't! ugh!

"Ko! Stop it now, kill this bug! Come on! You could have been showered, washed clothes, cooked breakfast and all kinds of stuff!"

"You're right I'm so sorry! I'm trying! It's just really hard."

"And what do we do when things are really, really hard or painful?"

"Count."

"Right, so let's count 'em down? Ready?"

"Yeah."

(together) "3, 2, 1!"

"BLAP!"

I smashed the life out of the bug! It dropped to the ground and laid lifeless. The paralytic wore off and I immediately breathed easily. I started smiling, shrugged off of the tension in my shoulders and commenced to cleaning the house. I cleaned up everything. I mean I started cleaning more than what I had planned, you know why? Because now I gotta clean up that dead ass bug on the floor! Ugh! I have to TOUCH it! No! even if I sweep it up...oh God, please don't let it move when the broom touches it, I will vomit!

I waste another 30 minutes or so cleaning unnecessarily because I need this trash bag that I am about to sweep this lifeless corpse into to be full so I can tie up the bag and put it outside! Once the bag gets full, I walk over to my dead terrorist and grab the broom. I know now I have to jab at it to make sure it's actually dead and not playing possum. I countdown quick and jab it! It doesn't move. I take the broom with confidence and sweep sloth slow to ensure this bug doesn't accidently go over the dustpan onto my hand or arm. After three minutes it's in my dustpan. I carefully pour it into the trash bag and quickly tie it up and throw it outside! And now all of the tension in my body releases and for the first time in over an hour I take a normal breath.

After this ordeal, I realized something about my life: most of the things I need to face are small. They may seem big. In fact, for what they are they could be big. But they are still smaller than me. They are still not as strong as me. They are easily disposable, but I fear. And that fear paralyses me so I don't do ANYTHING about it. Because I don't even know what it is, I'm facing completely. I know the gist, but not for real for real you know. So, I move through life making a lot of noise about this small thing, trying to get the attention of someone who will save me...who will kill this thing for me. I waste a lot of time, energy and resources "trying" when all I had to do was swing. Scary things, painful things might put me in paralysis but with a little coaching and a countdown I can stop putting the pressure on people whose job isn't to save me and save myself.

3...2...1

<u>Newly Lost</u>

It's interesting finding yourself after thinking you've been
found. How your beliefs can change on a dime.
My thinking has changed so tremendously.
Those close, believe for the negative.
I disagree.
Just more affirmed thoughts of lessons in life.

<u>Lays</u>

Intelligent.
Articulate.

You pride yourself in being stately and
maintaining your integrity while carrying
yourself with elegance.

But I still want my hot chips!
And yes, I suck my fingers clean afterward.

CHAPTER TWO
That Love Shit

Knew Not

It burned when it first hit me.

That's the first sensation I recall, before the full force of those scripted words' impact caused me to collapse back into my chair.

Air...

Breath I could not catch as that burn turned cool.

As my body turned numb.

Limp it went as I tried to process this feeling, this devastation. While my being did its best to recognize this unfamiliar sensation.

Heartbreak.

So this is what you feel like.

I've always known of your presence and will naively admit that I immaturely thought I'd met you before.

Thinking that time I'd wrongfully invested into rustic, unsophisticated persons should (at least at the time) be deemed heartbreak.

But they were not this.

This is earth shattering.

It came from nowhere.

Days before it was late night texts of separation anxiety.

In weeks past it was glorification of love shared.

Months ago it was the meeting of the halves that made us whole, that I was certain that its success solidified our never-ending story, our always, our lives.

How could it all change so quickly?

Your sentiment toward me.
I was finally certain that what I'd given was enough to have the thing that I never searched for...the thing I wouldn't reject having... had now apparently escaped me.
I understand the need for personal growth.
That necessity to choose you, trust me I do.
I just innocently thought I'd be beside you during that choice.

I'm angry and hurt but still I miss you.
The love I had.
The love I never truly knew.

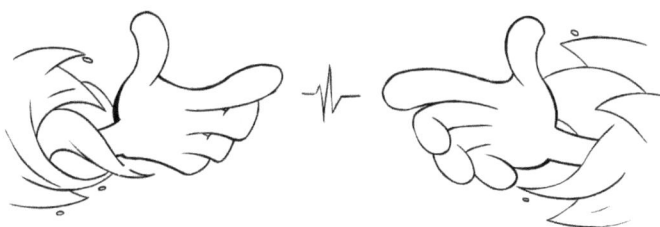

Busy Signal

You want my love, but me you want not.
Now if that ain't some confusing ass shit.

Its nearing month four and when I tell you that I am
exhausted.
I'm understating it.

You called me today and my heart stopped. Why does it
make me so happy to see your name, yet infuriate me so?

I didn't answer. I couldn't.
I've told you before...I have no words, no pleasantries to express.

So why call?

___Slant___

My truth is I'm in disbelief.
I'm in disbelief because every aspect of every vantage point in my
mind had us going in a totally different direction.
Family's meeting alongside birthday greetings instilled a
solidification of our maturation that you were my one.

Rose petal pulled: "He loves me not"

Timetable

You were in an affair.
I was in it forever.

Depiction

"it was real"

How could it be?
You now openly admit to
your lack of transparency.
Concede to me dishonesty
that was unprovoked
and unnecessary to justify a decision that
you chose to be our reality in a
Moment that I stressed the need for
brutal sincerity...
stating that
mistruth will never make sense to me.

But is telling of your character's
capacity that you would
make such a claim,
especially to me.

You cannot tell me what we could
be possibly when you moved so swiftly
To see if the grass was green,
which I find interesting considering
A number of your professings.
So what really were we,

Imaginary.

𝔖cene 𝔖tudy

He was of the theater and I recall thinking innocently once,
"I wonder if he would act with me."
Not knowing I was in the midst of a scene.

Priceless

Words don't seem to matter much to you
Not when they leave my mouth
Not when they come from my heart
Unless it feels good to you

Quick to call out but slow to listen
Quick to talk money and gifts but
Slow to pay attention
Which you already have
You don't have to work for that
Or maybe you've used it
Maybe you've exhausted it
By the time you eventually
Get to me
Pennies for my priceless thoughts

Nothing more
Nothing saved
Not for me
Not for us
It's used up
So, you give nothing
And expect everything in return
When will I learn?
That to vend
You must spend
Because at this point
You're getting the milk for free.

Blissed X

When were they just motions and no longer emotions that were expressed from your lips?

About how just my fingertips filled your body with bliss.

How I made it so easy for you to confide to…Where did it all go wrong?

According to you, you don't even know.

I think you did. You just didn't know how to stop playing the part.

Finality Clause

The arrogance of you.
To vehemently proclaim,
"I'm ready for this"
"I want this"
"I know what it is"
"I got this"

You didn't know!
How could you?

But I knew.
I knew way back when in the infancy of our begin that you truly
weren't ready for that relationship spin.
That constant rotation of loves subjugation, where one's strife is
also a part of my life.
That's love.
That's relationship.
But you were yet to be equipped.

Your adamancy shielded me visually from seeing your inability to
provide me true transparency.
You never fully submitted to the fact I was committed to your perfect
imperfections; my love ran deep.
I had no objections.
Your honor, I honored, I wanted it all!
Your good
Your bad
Your ashamed
Your insecure

I wanted every morsel of you.
But in my wanting there's only so much I can do.
For you have to be open, honest, and to trust, that part you
constitute.
But you didn't know how.

Even after years of affirmation you never had that revelation that my devotion to you had no equivocation.

Thus...your <u>eventual</u> final dictation.

"I'm not at a place to try at that level"

I knew it.

And it hurted.

But that honest explanation was all I ever wanted.

GrubHubs

After our end, I can't tell you when I will allow myself to go to Popeyes again.
I'll be honest though...I miss those damn biscuits.

<u>Simply</u>

You got what you wanted
And then you stop wanting
Who you got it from.
I get it.
But just admit
That's what this is.

Child's Play

I hate it had to come to this
But childish or not I had to unfollow.
I just can't keep watching you live your
Life without me.
Cause that's still a hard pill to swallow.
So

Yeah, I pressed that button
And I don't feel bad about it.
Renamed you in my contacts
"don't call back"
And I don't feel bad at all for that.
It's true.
It's how I got over you.

Below Surface

My truth is I'm angry.

I'm angry at myself because I knew better, and I knew I knew better.

I know that life is about experiences and personal challenges with feats to face.

But you convinced me that I was what you wanted.

In hindsight, I should have said no to that call.

I didn't save myself.

Instead, I initiated my own drowning.

<u>Selfie</u>

Proof of the truth of you and of all this I had to admit to myself and conclude.

Lies.

To do for self
Amongst oneself
To find yourself

<u>Self</u> however was not <u>whom</u> was sought.

Pacing

I guess in a way I should say thank you. Several months ago, I lost love. And it wrenched my heart. I didn't know what to think or feel and most importantly I didn't know how to heal. My mind was consumed with thoughts of whys and what didn't I see. I'm finally coming to terms with the notion that it was not me who is at fault. I'm not there yet, simply moving in that direction. It's hard. I'd given so much of myself. Half a year and the weight is still crushing.

But there is a lining of silver. I rediscovered an old love. One who was there long before you. Who consoled me in times of duress? Who encouraged when I thought of myself low? My belief in this love had begun to wane. Losing my last love, my biggest fear...not simply for it being "love" that would be lost, but I knew this was the first and only time I had truly given someone me. My insecurities, my fears, tears, fullness of personality non discreet, my family...truly me. I ran back into the arms of my old love, who had never left, but was simply waiting for me to see. My greatness, my poise, my strength and ability.

I've always been a slow burn. Measured, steady. I will move. But only when its right for me. I'm not concerned with the thoughts or where they think I should be. I've always done me. And granted I'm not in the place I know my future holds. It's imperative I allow the little things to lead to the big things and I will be eventually, certainly

Uncaged

What you said to me was like a bomb
But I didn't let it explode, No
I Luke-caged the hell out of that bomb
Held it between my palms and
Boom! Minimal damage.
A destructive thing
Reduced to a sting.

Optix

Am I supposed to want to talk?
To you?
In regard to the after a breakup?
Granted this "conscious uncoupling" was not dishes thrown or tire slashing, but that's because I'm not that type.
I've never understood that reaction.

Soooo me breaking your shit and hollering at you is supposed to make you want to stay with me???

Nah, I'd look at me crazy too.
So, my resolve is simple,
"This what you want? Understood. Let me grab my things."
And I'm out.
I'm not about to fight you to want to stay with me.
That's stupid.
I would want you to want to be with me and if you no longer have that need, then this is supposed to be.
Further having conversation is no necessity.

In addition to me no longer knowing you, I don't even know what "you" I would get.
I no longer tolerate partials or entertain pieces.
With hindsight being 20/20.
I see clearly, what I thought I'd seen clearly.

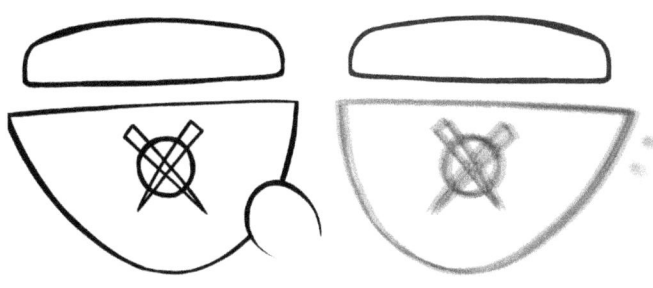

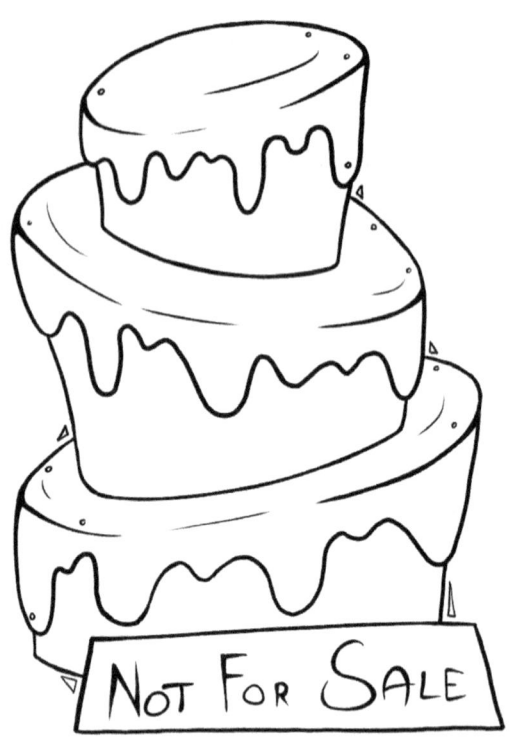

Exclamation

"Tha Fuck You Think This Is!?!"

Is to be my <u>new mantra</u>.
I am no cake to be eaten with.

Chic

You must've thought I would allow myself to be some type of consolation.

Why would I ever?

I possess an arsenal of intellect,
an abundance of debonair
with a tinge of The Astaire.

I have class beyond class.

Before you re-approach...study.

The One The Only

It was weird hearing my father refer to
My mother as his first wife.
"Nigga, she's the ONLY wife!"
And then I remembered I was talking to my dad.
"My bad."

Beware Of...

I wanted love like my mother and father.
The love like my Grands.
Not perfect, but solidly malleable.

Unfortunate I won't again allow that door to be creaked or
even a window slightly opened.
Ever.
My house is boarded, cordoned from the street.
"It's" not worthy of me.
I'm settled here.
Legs crossed, hands pleasantly in my lap.
With my guard dog resting at my feet.

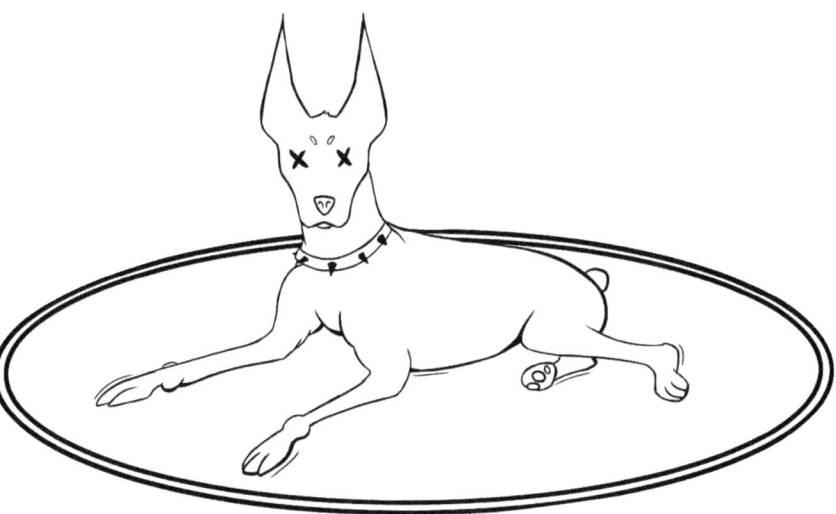

Abridged

How do we build an empire if we
Can't build a bridge between us?

Touch

I know you love me
No question at all
I feel it when you touch me
So gentle
It's like you say everything
You don't say with words
With your hands
You reassure me
But what of the times when we can't touch?
How do we
Love?

Risky Business

You took a risk without me
And risks are a part of love
so, I'm not mad at the risk
It's that you did it by yourself.
And when you take risks alone
it's not the tangibles you're risking.

You risk my heart
You risk my trust
You risk my belief

And you lean on my love with weight that feels unbearable.
When you risk things alone it breaks us
When we take risks together it binds us.
Even if we lose.
We bind in a way we never could have.
Because we did it together.

<u>Healing's Remorse</u>

So many things are right about you
Didn't even notice your flaws
Even when I finally noticed
I wasn't even bothered at all

Because your heart is pure your words are kind
And nowadays that's so hard to find
But there's a scar beneath your armor
You hide from me, won't let me see

That you're human,
and human is fragile
That you're hurting,
and hurting leads to pleading hearts
but pride won't let you heal

And I don't want to change you
But I don't think that I can love this way
And I don't want to hurt you
But I think you'll hurt more if I stay

So, I walk away

Give you space to be
Who you need to be
Give you time to see
What I see

<u>Cool Runnings</u>

You were my twenties wrapped up in a year.
You were the beginning of my freedom;
My pathway to being free in my body.

You were the one who made me see myself;
You were a mirror.

Made me feel good
about who I was period.
You loved me where I was.
You made me feel beautiful,
valuable, wanted as a woman.

And it's been amazing.

But,

We can't be...not because you're not good.
You are good.

Your mind will be what it is
until it's not.
You are going to think the way you do
until you don't.
And I won't grow.
I'll stop to help you
Because that's who I am.

And you need grace
You need space to grow
You need time to change
And I am done waiting.

<u>Optimist</u>

Heartbreak
Heartache
That shit, the soul it takes

Winter Solstice

I cannot tell you how much I have anticipated this day.
When my mind finally allowed me to allow you to fade.
Not that you're completely gone, I doubt that will ever be the case. However, for the first time in 1 year and 8 months I don't remember, remembering you.

I'm not sad, I'm not elated either.
But I am relieved.

A moment I thought to never come.
My mind was to forever be on defense at the expense of my hearts recompense.

The void once gapping finally starting to suture.

2nd Guess

Hesitate, Hesitate, Hesitate
I wonder...do we both hesitate?
Do we stall our expressions of care for fear of the return of
ultimate impending woefulness?
Cynics?
We can't be that.

<u>Budge</u>

We not anything...

I'm fine with that.

We may not become something...

I'm coo with that.

We chillin...

And if that's all this is to ever be...

I'll take that.

#improvement:)

End Anxieties Begin

You scare me.

My eyes well.
I want with you what I promised myself I would never allow again.

To care,
To Trust,
To possibly love.

You gave me your vulnerability willingly.
A question from me not asked.

You entrusted me with your sensitivities.
openly explicitly.

And my wall just crumbled.
I'm wanting you.

A desire I won't fight.

The Softening

I love, even when I don't love.
It's who I am.
Part of my being.
Your pain I feel and want to soothe,
I don't know why.
Your exposed self is breaking through.

"Us" isn't even in its infancy.
It's pre-consummation.
Pre-love.
Strong like.
Yet here I am.
Heart wide open after I barricaded it shut.

Touch(e)

There is a difference in the way you
Touch me since then
You touch me like you know me
Like you know every story
Every wound
Every laugh
Every scar
You touch me like I'm yours
Like you know all of my thoughts
Every single thought
Every single worry
Every single care
You touch me like you
made me
Like   you   formed
every curve
Every crevice
Every fold
Every hole
You touch me like we
share a soul

Everest

Brown Eyes
Brown Skin
Supple Lips
Your tightly coiled tresses.

All of you dazzles me.
To simply lay with you epitomizes life on high.
An ever-rising ascension to which I see no peak.

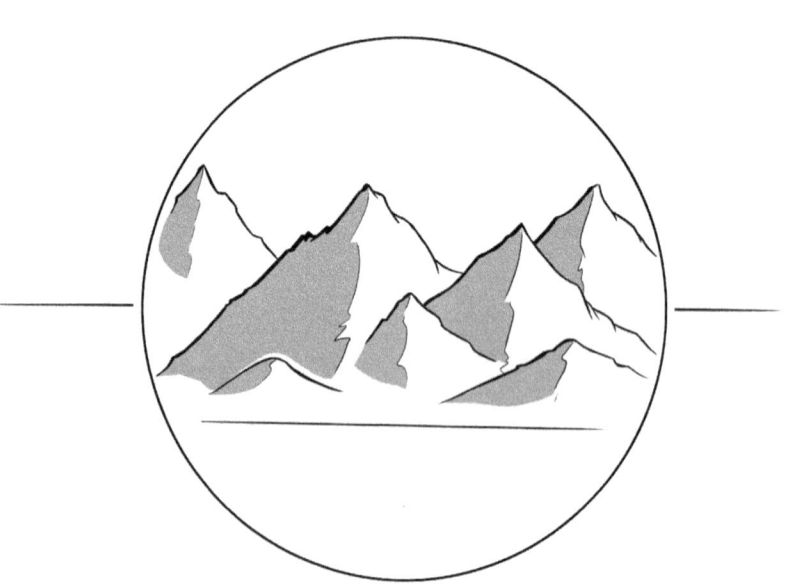

Simultaneously

It's crazy, because
This love is exactly what I prayed for
And exactly what I feared
At the same time

It is peace of mind
and a war of worlds
At the same time

It is hope infused
And exposed bruises
At the same time

It is joy on full
And grief unfiltered
At the same time

It is everything I need but wouldn't pursue
Or couldn't quite understand
It is everything I want, even when I don't know
What that is or what it looks like
At the same time

It scares me, and at the same time
Prepares me for whatever I might face
For whatever I might fear
For whatever I might fight

It annoys me, and at the same time
Employs me.
I work because of this love.

<u>Ebony</u>

It's not your body I want,

it's you.

I want the gaze of those deep browns.

The lushness of your mahogany lips.

The quiver your body elicits to my equip.

To feel your body tremble betwixt my fingertips places my spirit
in euphoric bliss.

But not because of those things physical.

Your mind moves my body.

Your heart feeds my soul.

It's not your body I want...

It was the music that solidified it.

Every song that played,

my heart swayed to a new rhythm.

The beats were different. The cadence fervent.

It crescendo-ed

Never to plateau and I don't want it to.

Fermata-

To hold

the note as long as one would like,

but certainly, longer than the written note value.

...I want you to sing to me

forever.

Home

There's no part of me
That I've given to you
That you haven't loved
That you haven't breathed life into.
No part that I've exposed that you haven't chosen to protect.

That you haven't loved.

Because you have never not loved me.
You were born with that space
With that place in your heart that you cleaned out for me.
This room that you've groomed so perfect to fit me and all of
my baggage;
You helped me unpack
And we sorted and sifted through my things.
Keeping little, casting much.

And I clutched
Gripping tight to what made me feel at home in your heart.
But you wouldn't allow outside things to define it;

Home.

You said we'd make it our own.
And when you said we
For the first time I realized I was included.
That you and I,
We are making our home.

I dropped everything
I stopped clutching
Started trusting
That from this day forward your heart is home and your arms
are safe space.
The safest place in the ethos for us.

So, forgive me

That Love Shit

For losing my key
For losing my way in these rooms
That you gave me.
You trust me with your heart
Because you want me to make it our home.

You want me to open the other doors and see what's in store.
You want me to sift and sort so we can keep what works and
pitch what's worthless.

You want me to use the keys
The keys I thought you were giving to lock me in...are the keys
to unlock everything.
Every part of your heart.

The parts you haven't even been to
The parts you don't want to journey alone.
You've asked me to make your heart OUR home

So, we can grow, and live our dreams.

You and me.

Our I do wasn't an invitation to a place I haven't known.
You opened up that huge heart of yours and gave me the tour.
Keeping some details to yourself
Because...well...
You know me.
You know I'd see a spider, or a house lizard and run...never to
look back.
But you confront what I see as harm and show me it's harmless.
You help me see, differently
My feeling safe has always been your priority
Because your heart is our home.

You want me to feel safe in our space
You want me to decorate
To fill up the place with my presence.
To highlight your essence

To balance your strength with my beauty.
To unearth the raw spaces and give them a name…a reason to exist, a purpose.

To put down my bags, unpack and stay for the rest of our days.
To join ways
To hang frames of pictures of moments we've captured to remind us of this space
Of our home in your heart.
And you're waiting for me to settle in…

And I've been fighting not realizing that this,

This thing that seems foreign
Is the very dream that I
Prayed to make reality.
And now that we're here
I fear…but you love
Until you ease me.
Until you feel peace
And we breathe

In…out.

This home we're making together
This home in your heart that starts our forever
And you're asking me to settle in

Well then…

Let US begin.

The Classic

Few people know this love

This love that crosses oceans

This love that stretches between continents

This love that is stronger than

distance from the moon to the sun

Over and over again

Day in and day out

This love that brings water in a drought

This love that brings calm in a storm

And cool in a desert

This love that oils the dry soul

This love that returns what was stolen

Fixes what was broken

Strengthens what is weak

Says everything right without speech

Without preach

Without pretense

Without politic

With and without logic

With and without science

With art

With start

To finish

This endless

Timeless

Priceless

Search the whole world just to find it

Wisdom's Brief

This love

exists

This love is bliss

This love that fuses souls one to another

This love that uncovers

This love discovers

Unearths

Births

Is worth

Life itself

A million times

This   love is yours, and   mine

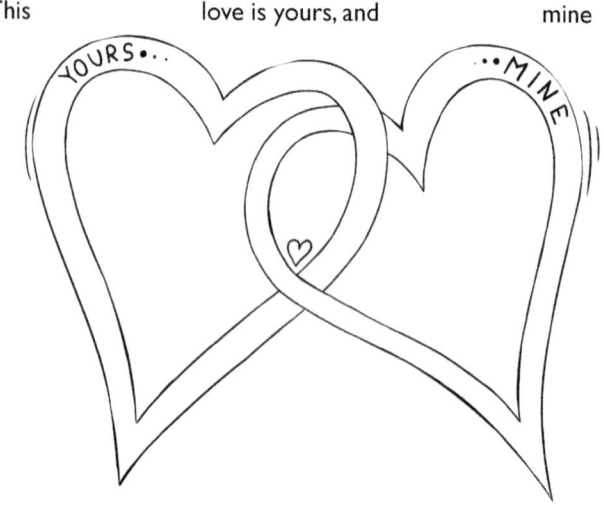

CHAPTER THREE
That Life Shit

Reset

My computer is the worst, like this mofo is like a stubborn papa. It does what it wants and has no care what you request: and dare your request require too much energy, that mug will just shut down quicker than quick. No explanation. Basically, my computer sits in its recliner with its remote and chips and responds when and how it wants. In its defense it is old, I've had it for five years...and it's a laptop...I think laptop years are more than dog years! Like for one year that's 15 years in laptop life.

So, my laptop is 75 years old and wants to be in retirement enjoying its life surfing the net and googling mindless things like how many licks DOES it take to get to the center of a tootsie roll pop? (I still want to know!) Also in its defense—much like the climate of America—I've used my computer much more in its retirement taxing the mess out of its income, not really taking care of it at all...but expecting it to work work work work work work...Put that on your agenda GOP...ijs...

I don't think...no, I know I didn't know what I was asking for when I started beggin' like Macon for a reset. In my mind when you reset things they fix. They work out bugs at the press of a button! Because that's what happens every time I reset my computer; it just...fixes. I push the button and everything active is shut down and then the screen goes black for a bit. That blackness...holy moly...

To fix it, everything goes dark first...

Over Being Under

I'm over it
over hearing it
over Feeling it
over seeing it
over every tiny torturous part of it
The heart of it
Beats my body like a boxer
Like a boxer who's bitter and looking
For revenge
Punching their poison into me with
Every Fist
Until I get
Intoxicated
Under the influence
Weighted down

Poem in A Minor

I told myself not to fall apart
But here I am falling
Here I am crawling to safety
But the net is broken

Wastin'

Frustration...something we all feel at some point, right? No matter its degree: mild, moderate or severe we feel it. And it never fails to have us acting a freakin' fool. Depending on the situation people might even stamp your frustration justifiable. In fact, MOST emotional responses are stamped "justifiable" as long as they aren't extreme, or prolonged and most important, negative (basically just don't kill anyone's vibe).

I mean if your cat dies and you're down for a couple of days maybe even weeks nobody's like "really! Get over the stupid cat!" Four years later though and you are still as sad as you were when it first happened...might raise a few eyebrows. If somebody says, "Hey beautiful" or, "Hey handsome," you might smile, giggle/chuckle, you may even blush. Nobody's going to say, "DON'T SMILE WHEN I COMPLIMENT YOU!" Now don't get me wrong. When you are happy, joyful, smiley, or surged with positive emotion prolonged or extreme, people might question it like, "What are you smiling about?!" or, "Nobody is that happy all of the time," but they won't stone you for feeling it. Annoyed by you maybe, only because you're reminding them of something they don't have.

Negative emotion prolonged and extreme disturbs us. Why is that? Weeeell negativity (stress) draaaaaaaaaains you like you just ran a marathon unprepared. What's crazy to me is that I didn't really feel the weight of this whole negative emotional overload personally until I found myself at work sitting in the corner on the floor of a bathroom (at this time I worked at a hospital...soooo). I was so frustrated that it had literally drained my strength to stand. So, I slid, slowly. The slow, dramatic, down-the-wall slide until I was sitting in the corner, knees pulled tightly to my chest, head in knees and tears running for their freedom down my cheeks.

I didn't even realize I was sitting on a dirty bathroom floor and honestly, I didn't care. To me, it had become a safe and private place to discard my waste. I mean...that's what it is, right? (Wastin') Think about it. People go to the bathroom for a couple of reasons...let me just say we relieve the stress of waste build up in our body. You're not thinking about a proper time to go when you have to go. I mean when you have to go, YOU HAVE TO GO! And you will excuse yourself from whatever it is to do it...and don't let there be a line! Whatever bathroom is open, here we come! (Oh, just me?). And what's even funnier is as dirty as most bathrooms are, they are probably one of the most peaceful places on the freakin' planet. Parents hiding from kids, spouses "freshening up" for one hour, employees taking a quick potty break, all happens in the bathroom...why? You can think clearly, you can breathe deeply (sometimes), you feel free, you feel light. And at the flushing of that toilet you know you are a little better than when you came in. I mean, you relieve stress, you freshen yourself and go about your business. We all do it. It's something we all share. At some point during the day, we all need to waste. Wastin' is a natural part of life! When you don't...stuff gets really uncomfortable really quick! So back to being on the floor of this bathroom...

I realized I was in dire need of a place to dump the negativity that was building inside of me. Maybe subconsciously my brain said, "Oh you need to dump waste? Bathroom, go to the bathroom!" And that I did. And as I sat there crying, reality hit me... (as did the sobering view of the toilet sitting next to me). I needed a place to waste for my heart, mind and soul because a lot of us don't have one.

I walk around every day without wasting the garbage I consume in my life. The negative comments, the misplaced negative emotions, the rejections, the straws that threaten to break my back, the daily dose of degrade and let's not even get on how I put myself down! I could tear a bathroom up with that alone!!! Most of the time it's not that something bad has happened. Being alive and encountering the world warrants waste management. If you eat or drink something, your body will use what it can and push the rest out. And if, so help you God, you so happen to take in something your body can't handle (something toxic) it will very aggressively push that something out of one of the ends of your body whether you want it to or not (disrespectful af!)! It's the same with the spirit and the emotions.

Now, I refuse to believe that the physical body is smart enough to regulate the waste (as long as it's healthy) it accumulates, and I'm not. It has been trained to do so. But like a baby, I waste on myself emotionally and spiritually without thought and then cry and whine about it, wanting someone else to come and clean me up when I am fully capable of doing it myself. Walking around just smelling up every place I walk into. Got people lookin' at me crazy and frowning up! Then I cop an attitude, like I don't smell my nasty heart and brain! I know if I smell it, you do too!! Or maybe I've grown so accustomed to the smell that I don't even notice it...either way...that stuff needs to be cleaned up!

I don't know about y'all...but when Tracy P (my mommy!) potty trained me, she expected me to go in the potty because I was trained to do so. Maybe I haven't been potty trained emotionally and spiritually, so I don't know how to rid myself of the waste I accumulate. Can I be honest? I know I'm not. In fact, I am still in the process (I think I'm wearing pull-ups now though :D) I didn't know how to deal with negative emotion. I took in all that life offered. I consumed all that situations and circumstances fed me...and I got sick and my heart was suffering because of it. I was slowly losing myself to toxic waste.

Man, people would be laughing, and I'd assume they were laughing at me. People could look my way with a weird face and start talking and I just knew they were talking about me. In my mind, the whole world was against me and I was ready to take them on! People would be like, "What's up Ko?" and I'd reply, "Nothing! Nothing is up over here! Everything is down! Down to the ground!" and stomp off. Before I knew it, I was snapping at everybody, including myself. I was crabby, I was irritable, I was depressed, confused, upset, and each of these negative emotions stacked on top of the other. When I was alone, after a day of smoozing and hiding, I was spent. And all I wanted was to feel good. A sedative...something...anything to numb the pain...something that couldn't judge me or say something about my decline. I didn't need to hear somebody tell me I was down, I knew it. I just didn't know how to get out of the hole...and I didn't want anyone else to know that I didn't know. Because I thought I was supposed to know. I mean I'm the nerdy know it all, I am supposed to know, right?

Afterthought

I surmised for the longest justifications for your actions.
Not fully realizing misdeeds in their immediacy.
Words said I no longer believe.
Pronouncements about our being.
Only to discover our being hadn't really been.

The Bullet

Can't be human
Can't feel especially not anything unpleasant
And I dare not get angry
That'll be your reason to cheat
And I'm already weak
That wouldn't just be the straw
It would be the bullet to the head
I didn't ask for

<u>Watershed</u>

No need to apologize while you cry.
Behind those eyes...lies.

#foolmetwice

"Begin a new?"
As what?
There is no trust.
Which I refuse to re-give.
I can't risk it.
You're a gun with
no safety...
You've shot me before.

Unworthy

I used to feel so proud
I used to want to loud it
Shout it to the heavens
And spread it through earth
But you made it worthless
You made it feel wrong

Closed?

For good or for not so good, he was able to start a
conversation that I had ended.

......open?

Requested Cover

"I'm not ready," you say.

But,
I gave you me beyond my own knowing's capacity.

<u>Slogan</u>

You asked me bout us "just fuckin",
essentially with nothing more.
Simply put... (insert **<u>new mantra</u>**)

WonderLand I

My dad and mom split after decades of marriage, after knowing each other for a lifetime

Since they were kids, and he split.

Not just from her but from all of us, all that touched that family circle.

And he helped make me. So, if my own creator could throw me away

Who are you to stay?

And you wonder why I wonder...

Why though I try, I can't seem to find the piece of my mind

That believes in me.

After being teased...no ...bullied, high key

Like why me?

I was a target that every loud mouthed, angry, bitter, too cool for school fool

Marked

So I thought...

If you can't beat 'em, then join 'em

And that was the day I learned to see myself through others' eyes

And to my surprise their vison wasn't much different than mine

They just used it against me...so I learned to use it against me

I learned to see myself as less than

At best when I'm lowering myself to please others

At best when I'm killin' myself to help my mother

Look out for my brother

And hope that my father finds a healthier cope

But I'm at the end of my rope...

And you wonder why I wonder

<u>Java</u>

I just need to feel good.
To uninhibit myself.
I've become so structed in my structure because life's structures
are so complex.
We neglect to disconnect.

Tweet My DM
Repost My Comment

...Fuck that! Can we talk over coffee?

<u>Murky Mirrors</u>

Put your phone down.
A simple request.

So you can truly see.

All these screens add this sheen of falsehood and nonrealities.
Concerned more with the image of you rather than the essence of you.

Likes and hashtags, views and repost,
are surely suffocating our psyche.

We scroll through feeds not realizing our starvation.
Searching for adoration from people broken.

What do we value?
What's really important?

That story you're posting I know is distorted.
For every life span consist of this...
good and bad, broken and put together.

But what makes life truly likeable is life being truthfully reflected.

Fill in the _____

"I didn't believe in my adversary until
the damage was already done.
I didn't believe in the weapons
so I didn't see them coming,
too busy running."

And some get stuck
in this loop trying.
Some refuse to live
so they choose dying.
And some surviving,
reach back to pull others out.
Out of doubt, confusion, delusion.

Because choosing is the difference between
You and things
Between you and dreams
Between you and
Shifts in reality.
You wanna be _____?
Great, fill in that space.

Concession Stand

I liked them, so....
I liked it.
Or was it that I wanted them to like me.
Passivity.
Don't concede.
Compromise.

<u>Give to Get</u>

Nobody gets it
Because you didn't give it to get.

New Pair

Seemingly it seems it's not what's legit and true.
In this age it's...
 what's new.

System

There is a system
And it works well
It's been working for quite some time
Well-oiled and maintained
Kept alive by the fire of fear
Coals of hatred and ignorance burn bright
And they'll never let it die

There is an equation in place
Factors that when added will always equal death
And death has many faces
(Racist, privilege, ignorance, cowardice)

Beating begot lynching
Lynching begot shooting
Shooting begot...more shooting
More jail time
Less life time
None of these are covered on Lifeline
Because the math
Doesn't add up
¾, not quite whole
And they say the
system isn't broke

They're right
The system was
designed
To find signs of life
and destroy it
Take chances and lace them

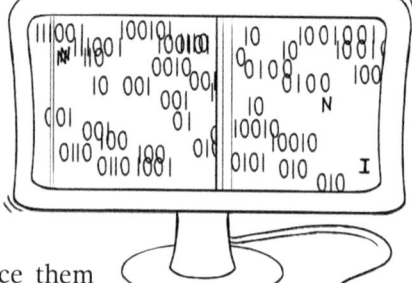

with illegal substance
Take opportunity and fill it with toxic chemicals
Make it cheap
And feed it to the community
The system is not broken

Slavery begot injustice
Injustice begot corruption
Corruption begot inequality
Inequality begot creative ways to take us back to first base
Slave

The system is not getting worse, it's getting stronger
Because what used to be illegal
Is now excused
What used to be heartless
Is now harmless

Regardless of what is said
The problem is not the system
It's the head
Your mind that you refuse to inform
That's what does the most harm
Your misplaced fear is the answer to every unsolved case
Of every face
Faced with bullets they don't deserve
For every word
Used to abuse power and enforce cower
This is the system they work hard to improve
It isn't broken
It's wiiiiiiiiiide open

State of the Human

But we're ALL human.
We all need.
We all bleed.
We all breathe.
Until the bullet rounds
And you hear the sound
Of arrogance
(you think you're better)
Of passed down sin
(parents didn't teach you better)
Of privilege
(you didn't earn that)
But you get it anyway
And take my right away
To be human

So, what is all...?
Y'all

Coined

"Ohh say can you see."
What is becoming our reality.
Hateful speech. As voices screech.
Do we even see one another?
Corners backed in with factions sectioned, we all gon' lose.
Cuz right now we're numb
To E Pluribus Unum.
"Out of many one."
Empathy.
It's time to try it.

Feng Shui

Life is a collection of events.
Both yangs in ying that shape your personality.
Things that altar your being down to the surest parts of you that can
cause you to be unsettled.

Little Foxes

Doubtful worry
Life in a hurry
No rest when we sleep
Little foxes
Cunning they are nipping at the root of our strength
Swift they are nipping at the root of our defense
Diligently biting at the base of our existence
Constantly clipping at our consistence
And their persistence decreases our resistance to fight
Little foxes
At first seem harmless
We don't shoo them away
We let them stay
And eat all the fruit of our garden
Killing our harvest
Now all this, hard work we've accomplished
Cease to exist
Because of little foxes
Weakening our immunity
Stealing our ability
Killing off humility
Leaving us no hope or peace
Yet we release
Little foxes
And let them run wild
Because they're small
Yet we trip and fall
Over little foxes

Wisdom's Brief

Unforgiveness
Bitterness
Emptiness
Foxes
Low self-esteem
Hollow dreams
Silent screams
Foxes
Rejection
Lack of affection
Ill protection
Foxes
Keeping us in boxes
That we don't fit in
Yet we give in
Because what used to be a figment
Is now the condition we live in
Foxes
That we ignore or chose to be blind to
Are the same little things that bind you
And grind you
To the lowest place
Self-hate
But you say I don't sweat the small things
When in fact
It was a straw that broke the camel's back
So beware
And be aware of
Small pains, small hurts, small things, small hate
They all carry weight
And drain health and grace
Be proactive, be on the watch
because what becomes big starts as a
little fox

Breathe

You don't think of how precious a breath is
Until there's none left
Until there is struggle
Until you wheeze or you gasp
Then perhaps...you get it.
And wish with all of your being
to breathe with ease
to not think
of every little step it takes
to get air in and out.

<u>Tell All</u>

How do I function in a world of "look at me" when my value
prefers privacy?
Can there be no success without full disclosured exposure?
Or can we not even have self anymore?

Loyalty

Loyalty sometimes doesn't serve me
But I can't not be loyal
It's in my DNA
I tried to pray it away
But that's useless
But what's useful
Is being loyal to things eternal
Because your temporary attitude
Will have me throwing the baby out
With the bath water
When I know
You're just trying to grow
Slow or fast it's not up to me
It's up to you

That's why I am loyal to things eternal
Because at some point
You'll find peace, you'll find joy
You'll maintain your happiness
You'll activate self-love
And cultivate self-worth
You'll put self-first, the healthy way
And the sting will fade

And the pain we endured in giving
Each other space will be replaced
With
Healthy, whole humans having each
Other's back
And that
I can always be loyal to.

<u>POV</u>

It's not your opinion that concerns me...it's your perspective that matters.

Because the lens through which you view the world shapes everything you say.

I won't argue opinions, especially baseless ones. That baseless opinion comes from a skewed point of view. Adjust the mirror, and the opinion will self-correct.

HOLLYWOOD

Lights. Camera. Action.
Distraction.

This world in which we move will consist of silhouetted truths.
Rather than ones presenting their true hues.
Smokescreens.
To veil your sensitivity because you are mired in masculinity.
"I can do it all!"
Until the levees break.
Washing you away to an infantile state.
Curled up into yourself,
knowing and even asserting the need for change.
But continuing to function all the same.
Only you can transform what it is you do.
So please...spare me your ridiculous excuse for why you have truly yet to.

Camera Shy

...LALA Land is a city largely composed of image. But what is an image without the negative?

(he)ART Therapy

Art has always been the place where I openly and freely feel and work out my emotion. It's where I feel safe.

I need shows like Parenthood and This Is Us because they let me know it's ok to feel. I can laugh hysterically or cry uninhibited rivers. I can be angry, afraid, depressed, worried, HAPPY...which usually leads to more tears lol or dances or songs or poems...art is feeling. It's feeling in the rawest way. It's feeling at its best. It's feeling awake, it's what reminds me that I'm human, which means I'm fragile and that's ok. Because it also means I'm strong as bonded super glue because humans have been around and evolving for a good while. Adapting and procreating. So, in the spirit of being human, I'll keep feeling, because that's how we adapt and create.

Tail Tucked

"You're too good to be true."
Why?
How unworthy we make ourselves.
That we truly believe we aren't deemed love, even when it's presented
bare naked in our face.
We instead turn to run afraid.

Little Baby Straw

It's never the big thing that breaks you, it's the straw.

It's always the

Little. Baby. Straw.

You survive five bullets to the heart and as you're recovering you get taken out by the common cold?!

A cough took you out, but not five metal fragments aimed at you at the speed of sound?!

Which I recently found, is faster than light!

Order of Operation

I used to think pain was the only thing that
could deepen my capacity
The only thing that could drastically change
me for good
But I misunderstood
Just like 2+2 and
1+3 and
2 squared and
-6 +10 and
X +2-6=4
There is so much more
And what I know now that I didn't before:
Power to be is in me, and no place else.

At Dim

My vibe is a groove.

That groove soothes me most every friday at bout 730 on a summer's
eve.
When the Sun has left the sky and instead of blue you see orange
and red soon to be purple hues.

My vibe is a groove.

It's one good hit of Cosmic Collision.
Which sparks my body to move.
Soulection peaking, speakers beating, my torso grinds intensely lit.
Body rolls, body ticks and dips.

My vibe is my soul.

All of my Children

I wanna be so good for you
Perfect, even though I know I won't be.
For you, I'd try my hardest
Because you deserve the best of me.

I mean I'll never not try for you.
There are nights where I cry for you
And you're not even here yet.
But I bet when you do
Those nights will multiply times two.

Happy and sad tears.
Tears of fear
Tears of joy
Tears of laughter
And after all of the tears
Or maybe during
I find the courage to love you into
the best version of yourself.
To guide you into the human you already are.

The star that already shines.
I know it won't be easy
Because I'll want you to need me
And you will for quite some time.
But it will change, and it will shift and eventually
The healthy thing would be you
Needing you.

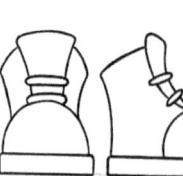

That Life Shit

I wanna accept that
Except that would limit my protection.
I'd have to expose you to grow you.
To invite outside influences
And allow intimacy with strangers.
To caution you of danger
But let you walk the tightrope
Over pits of dragons breathing fire.
Imagine

We'll spend so much time keeping you safe
And ensuring you're certain of yourself
And for your health
For your good
We have to cut the cord.
So you can be
And exist in your purpose
And trip over your own obstacles
And make your own mistakes
And blow out the candles on your own
Cake that you've made.

All by yourself.

Wishing for things born of your heart not mine
Pursuing dreams born of your soul.
Filling your own holes.
Feeling your own whole.
And I want you to...
I need you to

But right now...

I don't consider the who, what, when, where, why, how
I just want to enjoy the gift of the present
And be present for you as you unwrap
As you unfold
And I hope to give you my best
Because you deserve that...

<u>Little One</u>

Little one, little one so sweet, so kind
I've never told you
That you are worth more than diamonds
Even when you're insecure

You won't believe me no
Not for a while
Cause kids are mean, and they'll pick on things
That'll turn you upside down
Your failures and Growth
Own it all
It's all a part of you
And you're beautiful

So Slow down
You have time to grow
Don't you hurry
You'll know when you know

Don't you rush
Little one, little one
You have time
Don't you rush
Little one, little one
You have time

That Life Shit

You say you need to be bigger or smaller
You say things that lower your self-esteem
A little less
A little more
You change so much
Now you're unsure
And all you feel inside is
"I'm not good enough"

But hold your head up
You have time to grow
Don't you hurry
You'll know when you know

Don't you rush
Little one, little one
You have time
Don't you rush
Little one, little one
You have time

I know it's hard to live in your own skin
But it gets better you see
So, see it through

Don't ever make you feel less than
Because you're beautiful

Wisdom's Brief

Don't you rush
Little one, little one
You have time
Don't you rush
Little one, little one
You have time

CHAPTER FOUR
That Dream Shit

Vending Machine Dreams

I wanna look at my dreams
the way this little boy is staring at this vending machine
Like it holds all of the goodness, all of the keys
And he dropped to his knees to find them
To reach inside and bend and stretch and contort
His poor little arm 'til he damn near broke it...
Just to graze those Frito Lays
His little mind was in a haze
hoping his next attempt would be
Salty crunchy victory
He tried and tried
Stepped back a few times to re-evaluate his strategy
And look at me...
I get weak from one no
I suppose, Little girl in me is ready to try again
She's been waiting
Eagerly anticipating the green light
to stick and twist and contort her poor little arm
right into harm's way
To get what she came to take

Unfit to Dream

I dream... But not big, not extravagantly

I put limits on what I see

Cause my vision is blurred

Obscured

By words I haven't processed

By lessons I haven't applied yet

By life I haven't given time to

Mind you, I'd believe it if it was you dreaming

So, it seems

I'm unfit to dream

But how do I get in shape?

How do I lose the weight

of dreams deferred?

Horizon

At the precipice of my truths and I'm scared.

Beyond that plateau is where my life resides.

Truths once released, my soul's greatness will be magnified.

<u>Night Visions</u>

Practicality or emblazoned battles for the dreams we seek.

The visions of us we want to be.

A willingness to fight the tide that strides to dismantle our fortitude.

Resolute dream believers we are, and what we will always be.

Wisdom's Brief

I live in My Head

Literally...every dream, everything
I've ever wanted to accomplish has come true
I rehearse it--no--replay it in my mind
And right before it ends, I rewind
Because if it ends...then
I actually have to play it out
Play it loud
Headphones off
Unplugged
And instantly all of the noise
Pierces the silent film
And its sound is not on the same track
This track's sound is doubt
Life stress, lifeless, like less...
And the volume is loud
No blend, no level, no mix
Just sticks and stones
Just broken bones
Just words that have hurt me
Just words that haunt me
Taunt me, even.
Laughing at my feeble breathin'
My weak ass dreamin'
My mouth moving
my heart wounded
my mind...

playing the same wins
the same scenes
the same dreams
the same things I'm praying for

That Dream Shit

clearing my energy for
raising my temperature
cleaning my aura, my chakras
and every other oddball thing
just to fuckin' dream while I'm awake
to convince my heart the real isn't fake
the real isn't fake
the real isn't fake
it just takes...a while
is that a smile?
Yeah because though I get lost in space
Though my mind race
Though time plays
Though I feel I have no say
There IS a way
if I start talking
if I start walking
if I start...
Get out of my head

Get out of my bed
And live while my eyes are open
And rest when I'm asleep
And dream while I'm awake

And...

The Pursuit of Legacy

It's not about success, it's about significance.

Me

Me. Always looking through the window watching the world, rather than being of it.

__Loudspeaker__

We often forget the shoulders on which we stand.

The bodies that were broken.

Whose stories have gone unspoken...what were their dreams?

Did they star gaze about the days where their bodies could just lay

And not be used for profit and pay?

Often left in unmarked graves...we must honor them.

For they couldn't have foreseen the life that is our being.

So, what is owed, is that we be bold.

Reckless in our fearlessness, move with no constraint.

While their persons were quieted, our voices won't be faint.

Nexus

There's beauty in the hustle

Push

There's beauty in the muscle

Flex

Into the unknown that awaits you next

Cause that next is

The nexus

Of your nest egg

Being nested

And hatched

Into the new

Into the you

That sees

Beauty in the struggle

Beauty in the hustle

Legacy's Whisper

Time waits for no one.
Don't drag your feet through muddy waters.
Run like the waves in the ocean.
Rise like the tide.
And know if you keep running, you'll be alright.

A Woman's Love

I am like this woman I have never known.

So much like her that he sees her in me.

The love he felt from her heart, he feels through me.

I am surprised,

Not because he easily identified it.

Why would he not?

He knew that love for years, decades even...

He was created in that love.

Born of it, raised in it.

That love allowed him to be the man he is today.

And then It went away.

It died and a little space inside of him went black...

I brought the light back.

That Dream Shit

Cleared the cobwebs, dusted, swept, and made alive.

A space he left to die.

Now that space is his literal vibe;

He said so himself.

And when I asked what made me the right fit,

Why he picked me he said simply:

"You are the love of my life."

The love that gave him back his light.

The love that she gave him and raised him in.

The love I was scared to reveal.

Scared to give but, brave enough to show.

Brave enough to live out.

The love I've shown

reminds him of this woman I have never known.

This woman who gave me the greatest gift without knowing me at all.

This woman who visited me on such a special day

Just to say, "Thanks."

She thanked me.

For allowing her love to flow through me to her son.

She challenged me to love him fully.

To accept him fully.

And then she blessed me.

Blessed us.

And sealed it with a hug that felt like heaven.

Rightfully so since that is her home.

She just came to visit this woman she's never known

To assure her the heart she now lives in is her own.

Bashful

Fear of your greatness is real. Sincerely.

I now refuse to let that fear stagnate.
To reveal the honest you to the world is hard,
worse though would be living a life with inhibitions.
Just be me.
Unabashedly.

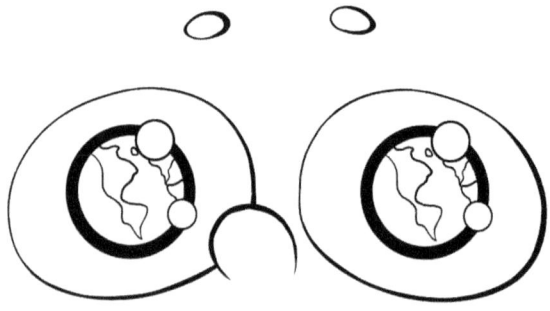

Jupitar's Titan

Who's watchin?

It doesn't even matter.

It's content and time spent.

Be hell bent N constant.

No mercy, just word free.

In passion I fashion,

compassion with word's strength.

I will blast in...BLAST'N!

No way?

Then make one.

Lucid Dream

I dream of red farm doors and wrap around porches

with a swing chair...

Of a baby grand near a wall of books

and a nook to read in...

A huge floor to ceiling window for fresh air to breathe in

A house with three healthy, happy children

and a healthy, happy husband whose businesses are growing

His pride glowing, our love growing...

Of Grammy and Oscar plaques lining the walls

of a professionally built and equipped studio

fully loaded with gadgets a plenty...

Of many memories of moments that make history

And solve mystery

And heal misery

And give energy

And yield ministry

To many hearts of starving artists

That Dream Shit

To current and future legends...

Of meetings with major clients enlisting me

as a key in their visionary pursuit...

Of money in the amount of influence and impact
on grandeur scales

Of wealth and health

Of a dancer's body with long, wild healthy
dreads

gracing my big head

Of trips with friends that stamp moments into
my mind forever

Of uninterrupted time with my lover to
rediscover the joy we have in each other

Of life I guess, nothing less.

CHAPTER FIVE

That Faith Shit

Charting the Uncharted

I would never have chosen writing. NEVER! If I'm going to tell a story—mine in particular—I'll just tell it. I'll tell different stories as they fit in different situations. In an interview I'll be candid and open, and I'll tell them whatever they ask me, because much like an open book, I'm...well...open. 😊 The misconception though, is that an open book requires no effort. BUT...it does. If a book is open, you still have to pay attention to the page. Look at the words and actually read them. Take them in. And if you so decide to want to know more, you have to use your hand to turn the page and repeat the first few steps! I don't mind telling my story, it's writing my story that's hard. You see, I'm reliving this with every character space I type. The good, the bad, the ugly, re-lived! And that's the hard part.

It's why I sit most days in front of my computer, staring at it. I stare at the blank page wondering if courage will help me carry out this daunting task. Sometimes I let courage do what it is designed to do, push us through the fear...other times I cower. But not this time.

This time, this project—this book—I'm travailing through it. Because I know how ridiculously hard this is. Journeying through your own heart. It's what pushes me through the block. It's what motivates me past fatigue. It's what coaches me through the pain. I say to myself, "Yes this is hard, but if you do this, other people will know they can, too." It will no longer be uncharted territory. It will be territory that we cautiously navigate until debris is cleared and paths are opened.

<u>Safe-</u>

"Protected from or not exposed to danger or risk; not likely to be harmed or lost."

Apparently this is how I make people feel.

A nurturer, it's engrained in me.

If I see beings in need of deeds of good, of warmth and love.

To listen, even at their silence.

To speak even when they're gasping in their own loudness.

To just be there.

It's simple... If you care, show you do.

I do.

My safe, however, alludes.

Steady being broken in two.

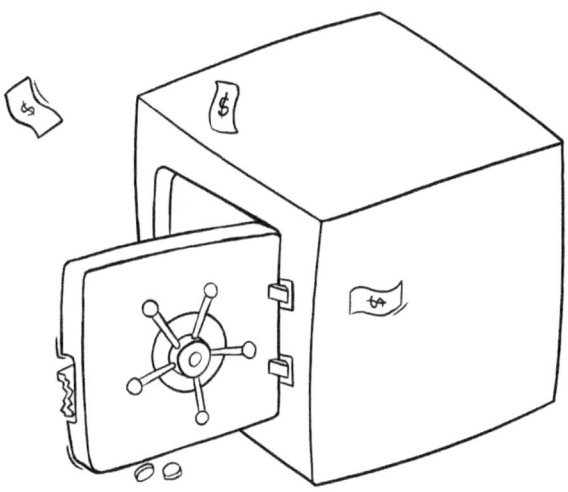

Living While Alive

There were days when I hated to see

The sunrise

To open my eyes and realize I'm breathing

Because life had no meaning

Until it did

Until the dread became dream

And the dream became steam

And the steam became things

I'd only imagined

Now they happen on a regular basis

And I'm faced with

The great joy of living while alive

And now when I open my eyes

I realize I'm breathing

Every breath full

Innnnn and Ouuuuut

<u>Solar Flare</u>

How do I find me when
I was lost here?
Your own reflection
unreflective of you.
A shelled exterior
with cracks of radiant
luminescence bursting to burn through.

Difficult?
Yes...hard, life is.
Exhausting it will be.
But oh, the beauty of
the depths of your dark.
Which reveal rays
of light leaving
your Sun set to reach the world.

Sincerely,
Shine...
Scorch the Earth

Embers

You never saw this coming.

Death.

Apologize!?

He knew what that meant.

You had the fight to fight the fire, but not the fire to fight your life's fight.

"No!" to your sorry.

She needed...

We wanted...

you.

Wonderland 2

You wonder why I wonder
Why your absence causes question
Causes pause...why I am at odds
Why my heart holds its breath
Why I can't give a FUCK about it

Because I'd quit
If I allow my feelings too much say
I'd part ways and never look back

So, I give voice to my spiritual being
To things unseen
Because what sits before my eyes
Makes me feel less alive
Less wanted
Less cherished
Quite embarrassed
If I'm honest

And I don't want this to be our story
So I surrender all to a glory
Higher than this

Wilt None

The doctor unmasked as if he were this empathetic reaper.

Relaying the words that he was no longer my father's soul barer.

The feeling I know that ripped through your body you could never fully convey.

But the collapsing of his brothers around you,

expressed the words you could not.

But you...you stood firm as an evergreen that never sheds no matter the season.

Although inside as you've told me.

"I wanted to rip that room apart beyond recognition."

Catch and Release

Take a breath...a deep one

Hold it

But not tight

Let it fill you up

But not full

Because it flows

It's not stagnant

In and out

Eb and flow

Catch, release

Atlas

Our sky began to fall, and you held it up.

You planted your feet, shoulders wide, heels dug, and straightened your back to embrace the full burden.

Tears rolling down your cheeks, you held your head on high with poise and dignity, gritted your teeth while life's new storm raged around you.

Our sky had fallen, but you fought and pushed and forced it back up.

Lunar

Us and now just you.

How overwhelmed you must've felt.

I so remember your stepping out for those late-night drives.

To let out late night cries...

You didn't want us to see your fears, or struggles as you fought ferociously to pull us out from beneath the ruble.

And being the bad ass you are, you built a house on top of it.

Purge

Maybe it's just God's way of
Clearing paths for me to be ok
Be on my way
To something bigger
To something better
To...

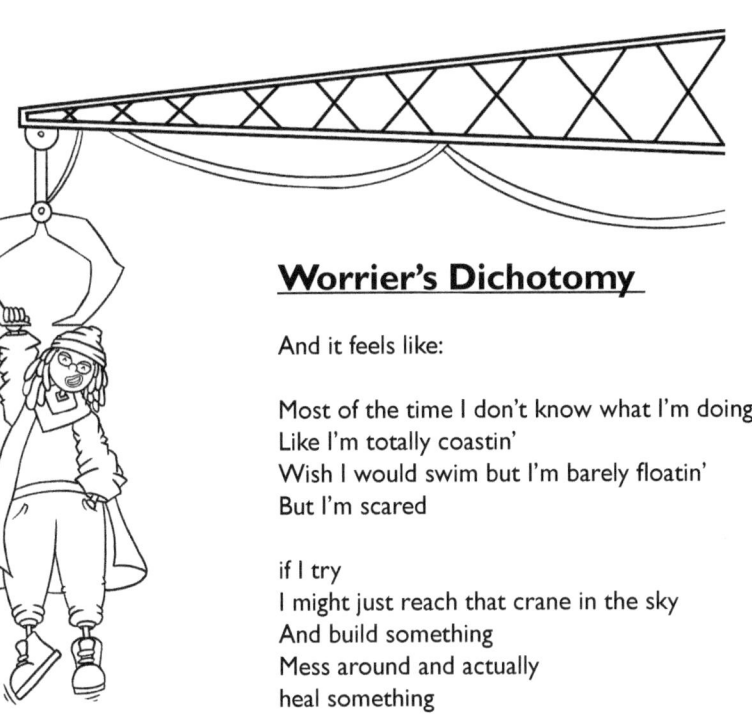

Worrier's Dichotomy

And it feels like:

Most of the time I don't know what I'm doing
Like I'm totally coastin'
Wish I would swim but I'm barely floatin'
But I'm scared

if I try
I might just reach that crane in the sky
And build something
Mess around and actually
heal something

But I don't always wanna work hard
So I drink it away
I eat it away
Push it away

But that's a dangerous game
Time to aim
I'm tired of missing
Tired of wishing
I know I can do this
I know I can win
if I just choose it

So
I choose it

Furtado

Like a bird with a wounded wing
I moved.
Carrying everything
And every string
That had me bound
But today I found strength
A strength that can't be broken
Because it wasn't given
I live in it
From inside it pours
More and more
Until each mask is gone
And each task is done
And what's left is healed
What's left is sealed
And finally filled
With things I can finally feel

No Faux
(Freedom)

I want to represent freedom, because love at its greatest is that. Think about it...and this is from the (I'm going to use the C word) Christian perspective, but just hear me out lol.

John 3:16...this is one of the "famed" and "beloved" scriptures, right? It's one of the first ones you learn as a Christian. And it says: "For God so loved the world that he gave a bunch of rules and regulations to control it, and whosoever follows them will not perish but have everlasting life." ...that's not what it says AT all...but that's how we've interpreted it. That's how we've used it. We've turned something beautiful into something very ugly and what was a very simple ticket to freedom has become a complicated glasshouse of manipulation.

That scripture actually says: "For God so loved the world that he gave his only begotten son, that whosoever believes in him will not perish but have everlasting life." Let's think on that...

I've heard many wonderful breakdowns of this verse—like life changing breakdowns. And I hope to add to that group by saying this...

This major act of love is a key to freedom...if you can believe that a way has already been paved for you. That this thing you struggle with, this issue is already worked out you just have to stay present long enough to work toward it, you would believe your way into the freedom that has been waiting to embrace you.

God doesn't love us into a box, he loves us out of them. The entire Bible gives story after story after story of him freeing people...how did we miss that?

Love is the ultimate dose of freedom; the breeding ground of flourishing and nourishing. And if that's not the experience you're having, then it's not love that you're getting. It's manipulation dressed in love's clothing. Run. Fast.

<u>Impressions</u>

I'm...
My Mother's Will.
My Dad's Gallantry.
My Grandfather's Charisma.
My Grandma's Heart.
I got my Swag from my Big Bro.
My other Brother
made me Dutiful.
I'm them in Reflection.
A thankful mold
you created in me.

<u>Resonant Trust</u>

Words are hollow when actions don't follow
They don't resonate, they echo distant.
But I listen...
hoping for a resonating that sort of lingers
It's like fingers being super close to touching my hand
But they stand, at a distance.

But I listen...
Anticipating the landing that shakes in turbulent flow
It's like water that won't go because it's damned
And it will only flow to the path of least resistance.

But I listen...
Praying for a wave to bust through
Because I trust you.

This Girl

I met a girl she was just sixteen
She has her whole life figured out
No fear at all
Just struttin' on em
Confident
She knows what she wants
And any ball you throw her
She knocks it out
Any lie you tell her
She sniffs it out
And she couldn't care less if you like her
Because she likes herself
And she's not interested in being
Anyone else

<u>Me Two</u>

I wear my heart on my sleeve
And it's not easy
Believe me
If I could wear it anywhere else I would
But it's who I am

Belief's Compass

We don't have a belief problem.
We have a direction problem.
Our faith is always there, it's just a matter of how
We choose to direct and invest it.
Choose well.

.

Stay Main

I was acting as accompaniment, when I, too, am the presentation.

About Griot

Two very different paths led two very different people to the same place: the land of opportunity (Los Angeles). Although they did it different (one dropping out of college and working an unfulfilled job, the other graduating and working in an unfulfilled career) their journeys led them through similar situations, obstacles and victories. Their life experiences and truths fuel the content of their storytelling. College brought them together and pursuing their passions in life keep them together. Bosco, the passion driven prose and Kay Oh, the purpose driven poet make up the drama-comedy that is Griot (gree-o).

 weare_griot

About KO

You know those kids that can't sit still? The ones that make noise when they shouldn't? The ones who sit around asking a million questions sponging up "grownfolksbusiness" until they are sent off to bed? Kay Oh (K.O) is still that kid.

She's a little bit country, a little bit pop and soul, and a lot of 24K magic!K. O. isa musician producer/composer, and poet. Sheknowsthe power arthas; She'switnessed it in herown life and hasbeen apart of sharing, expressing and cultivating it in the lives of others.From early days in church to rockin' stages in many places;simply put, art has helped hertranscend boundaries and limits, and in turn be anadvocate and ambassador for that same liberty in others.